MOUNTAINS OF AMERICA

MOUNTAINS OF AMERICA

PAUL KING
Photographs by J. A. KRAULIS

Crescent Books
New York

This 1992 edition published by Crescent Books,
distributed by Outlet Book Company, Inc., a
Random House Company, 225 Park Avenue
South, New York, New York 10003.

Printed and bound in Hong Kong
By Book Art Inc., Toronto

ISBN 0-517-06987-3

87654321

PAGE ONE:
Denali is the ancient Athabascan Indian name for Mount McKinley. (BRIAN MILNE/FIRST LIGHT)

PAGE TWO:
Yellowstone National Park's Grand Canyon of Yellowstone is a 1,200-foot-deep gorge with waterfalls.

PAGE THREE:
A view from Owens Valley of the east escarpment of the Sierra Nevada, the highest and most rugged mountain barrier outside of Alaska.

PAGE FOUR:
A shoulder of Mount Marcy, and Mount Colden reflected in a pond in the Adirondacks, New York.

PAGE FIVE:
Wilson Peak, part of Colorado's Wilson Mountains, has an elevation of over 14,000 feet. (RICH BUZZELLI/TOM STACK & ASSOCIATES)

CONTENTS

MOUNTAINS OF AMERICA

*"Just as a universe is violently constructed with
a subtle beauty of form, mountains born of fire
and force portray a similar magnificence."*

— Immanuel Kant

A view of the North Cascades from Washington Pass.

*(Opposite) Mount Hood, at 11,235 feet, is the highest
peak in Oregon.* (WARREN MORGEN/FIRST LIGHT)

MOUNTAINS ARE NATURE'S MOST impressive creation. They command the eye and enlarge the soul. They dominate the globe like nothing else except the oceans. Other planets have huge volcanoes, but mountain chains exist only on Earth. The Rockies and Appalachians are unique within the solar system.

Since mankind began, mountains have been the pathway to heaven and home to the gods, sacred to religions throughout history. Noah's ark came to rest on Mount Ararat. Moses climbed Mount Sinai to receive the Ten Commandments. The Greeks allocated Mount Olympus to their bickering deities. Mohammed saw the archangel Gabriel on Mount Hira. Africans worshipped the god N'Gai on Mount Kenya. Incan altars stood atop Andean peaks, Tibet's Mount Kailas was holy to both Hindus and Buddhists, and the Nepalese worshipped the gods on Mount Everest. The Japanese considered Mount Fuji sacred, and St. Patrick went atop Croaghpatrick to pray. Monasteries still stand on the highest summits where holy men are nearest heaven.

Since mountains often separate nations, alpine passes have been crossed by such conquerors as Attila, Napoleon and Hannibal—with his 46,000 freezing soldiers and 37 bewildered elephants. Yet to alpine peasants beneath the peaks, the spirits dwelling in the summits were always fearsome. Thunder and lightning were the war games of the gods. Until 200 years ago mountains were mainly shunned in horror. In the late eighteenth century, when the famed Swiss

Yosemite Valley with Bridalveil Falls and Cathedral Rocks on the right, El Capitan on the left.

scientist Horace Benedict de Saussure tried to scale Mont Blanc, the locals warned him it swarmed with demons and dragons. In America, August Kautz, planning an attempt on Mount Rainier in 1857, wrote that "Indians were very afraid of it." They believed an evil spirit lived "in a lake of fire" on its summit. Yet, regardless of superstition, the natives had cause to dread summits, for death came swiftly from freezing cold, landslides, volcanoes and slamming avalanches.

And mountains still kill. In the Second World War, tens of thousands of Austrian and Italian troops died beneath avalanches in the Dolomites. In 1962, a 3-million-ton block of ice plunged 9 miles from a glacier in Peru, crushing nine villages and 3,500 people. In 1970, an avalanche from the same mountain took 70,000 lives. In 1985, a volcano in Colombia erupted after 400 years, burying 23,000. And America has not been spared. In 1980, after 120 years of lying dormant, Washington's Mount St. Helens erupted, killing more than 60, scorching forests and blanketing four northwest states with volcanic ash.

These devastating volcanoes and earthquakes remind us of the forces still boiling within our planet, the forces that formed the mountains in the first place: recurrent slow-motion paroxysms that squeeze solid rock like clay in the fist, grinding and contorting the Earth's crust, lifting landscapes and sea levels to new heights.

Mountains have changed so little in man's history that we consider them symbols of agelessness, of eternity. Yet, like the Earth itself,

A view from along the crest of the Blue Ridge Mountains.

they've altered dramatically over the eons. During billions of years, entire mountain ranges have risen and eroded. And in time the summits that now crown Earth's surface will crumble, while other ranges will rise. The face of the globe, if we don't destroy it, forever changes.

What makes a mountain? Until this century, nobody knew. In 1694, Edmund Halley claimed that Earth had passed through a comet's tail, which caused the Biblical flood and "the heaping up of mountains." In the eighteenth century many believed that gasses escaping from Earth's interior inflated mountains like giant balloons. Others thought the Earth was shrinking, and mountains were formed like wrinkles on old apples. John Beaumont thought that "mountains

might be occasioned by fermentation, after the manner of leaven in dough," while Isaac Newton observed that if one poured beer into milk, the resulting curd did resemble mountain shapes. Yet even as far back as 1620, Sir Francis Bacon observed how the Old and New World continents could fit together like pieces of a jigsaw, and so, in fact, they once did.

But amazingly, it wasn't until the 1960s that most scientists finally acknowledged how the pieces split apart. Today, geologists overwhelmingly agree on global plate tectonics: the theory that the continents and ocean basins slide around on crustal plates, and earthquakes and volcanoes rumble out where plates pull apart or grind together.

For 4.5 billion years, the Earth's configuration

The Gore Range, part of the Park Range in northcentral Colorado, has peaks with elevations over 13,000 feet.

has constantly changed. Yet the world as we know it today took on recognizable shape some 200 million years ago when most of its total landmass was packed together in an equatorial supercontinent called Pangaea ("all the land"), surrounded by one vast ocean. But slowly, on its plates, Pangaea began to break up, like ice floes in the spring, the massive floes resembling today's six continents. Propelled by forces churned up from the molten sea on which Earth's surface floats, they slid through the eons to their present sites. In the process, new oceans were formed.

The plates on which the continents ride were created from molten rock welling up from a rift in the world's greatest mountain range, the Mid-Ocean or Mid-Atlantic Ridge. More than 46,000 miles long, and with peaks rising 13,000 feet above the ocean floor, this subterranean network of mountain chains envelops nearly as much area as all the continents combined. (The oceans cover 71 percent of Earth's surface.) Other subterranean mountain ridges stretch 24,900 miles long, 2,500 miles wide and 2.5 miles high, often rising above the surface to form islands. But most oceans hide the plate edges (ranging from 43 to 62 miles thick) which move through these undersea ridges and trenches at speeds from 0.4 to 4 inches a year.

Running through the center of all these ocean ridges are deep rifts that form the boundaries of the plates on either side. When molten rock from the rifts shoves the plates apart, boiling lava gushes up through the gap. This either cools and hardens into new crustal rocks, which widen the oceans, or forms underwater volcanoes, which often produce islands. But when they collide,

The snow-covered summit of Mount Baker in the North Cascades has an elevation of 10,778 feet.

they creat mountains from the wreckage.

When plates shove together, one plate is forced to grind down beneath the other, a process known as subduction. As the descending plate sinks into Earth's hot mantle, it melts to form fiery "magma,"which rises through the overlying plate to the surface, thus fueling volcanic mountains, such as Washington's Mount Rainier. While the Romans blamed volcanic explosions on the angered blacksmith god Vulcan, the blasts occur when gasses and steam trapped in the molten magma expand, and hurtle "volcanic bombs" in the air. The planet has given birth to 850 active volcanoes, most concealed by oceans. Yet while many today are dormant, an average of 20 to 30 still erupt yearly.

Dome mountains are also formed when the molten magma rises from the Earth's mantle,

but instead of erupting through surface volcanoes, the magma pushes up the overlying rocks to form a great arched dome. Then the magma cools and hardens into granite. An example of dome mountains is the Black Hills of South Dakota.

When continent meets continent, however, the clashes are even more titanic. Since neither plate edge can easily descend into the denser layers of the earth, they bulldoze the rocks on the seabed between them into giant wrinkles, which continue to rise over millions of years. India, for instance, is still being inexorably driven under the south flank of Asia, pushing the Himalayas up about an inch every five years. It also explains why sea fossils are found atop Everest. Such peaks, including the Alps, Appalachians and part of the Rockies, are called fold mountains.

12

A granite peak of the eastern Sierra Nevada, California.

Plate movements are also responsible for those mountains that form when moving plates split massive rocks in their paths, creating deep fissures, or faults, in the Earth's crust. Huge blocks of rock tumble into these faults to create steep-sloped rift valleys, or are hoisted upwards to produce great fault-block mountains, such as California's Sierra Nevada and Wyoming's Teton Range.

While scientists have only belatedly accepted their existence, plates have jockeyed for position on our globe for the past billion years. The Appalachian mountains, for instance, are remnants of collisions between North America and Eurasia-Africa some 350 million years ago. Yet the clashes (as San Franciscans can testify) haven't ended. For Earth alone among the planets has continuing tectonic activity.

And just as continents separate and rejoin over millions of years, and as plates move about and split apart, mountain chains are thrown up and eaten away—for while plate collisions push mountains upward, gravity inexorably pulls them down. This is due to the armies of erosion, as forceful in their way as any earthquake. Over time, the ancient Appalachians have been worn far lower than such younger, 65-million-year-old ranges as the Rockies. Generally, the highest ranges are those most recently formed. An excellent example of erosion mountains is New York's Catskills, which resulted from the grinding away of sedimentary rock—such as limestone, dolomite and shale—deposited on the surface from ocean beds. (The other two types of rocks within mountains are igneous, such as granite, which solidified from molten rock mass beneath

The dead but handsome gnarled trunk of a bristlecone pine in the White Mountains of California.

Pinnacles on ridge in the San Juan Mountains, Colorado.

the Earth's crust, and metamorphic, which was produced by heat, pressure or water.)

The forces of erosion start, of course, with rain. An average mountain stream washes down 1,000 cubic feet of dirt and pebbles in a year. Frost is another cause of erosion, since the ice that forms in crevices occupies nearly one-tenth more space than the original water. This subsequent swelling splits the rock apart, causing rock slides. Frost also forms glaciers, those massive, moving behemoths of ice that slice down mountain valleys, their surfaces littered with shattered rocks, which act like sharp cutting edges. Then there's wind, which scours alpine slopes like sandblasters on skyscrapers, for mountains are not only the wettest, but also the windiest places on Earth. The world's highest wind speed—231 mph—was recorded atop Mount Washington.

Still, while erosion is usually snail-paced, it can change a landscape in seconds. When rainwater is absorbed by plant roots, the weight of the soil increases dramatically, causing landslides. (In 1920, the worst landslide in history buried 180,000 Chinese.) Mountain avalanches not only carry snow, but tons of soil, rocks and trees down slopes. So do earthflows, the sudden movement of topsoil, often caused by water mixing with loose volcanic ash. (A 1985 earthflow in Colombia killed 25,000.) Volcanoes not only spew out lava and stone, but clouds of ash and gas that destroy everything in their path. (Mount Pinatubo in the Philippines had such an eruption in 1991.) Yet for all their destructive power, volcanoes alone have also been constructive. By releasing gasses and water vapor from rocks,

Wyoming's monolithic Cirque of the Towers were sculpted by glaciers.

they helped create the atmosphere and oceans. Volcanic soil is also considered the world's most fertile. But either feared or revered, volcanoes exist on every continent except Australia.

North America rests entirely on one enormous tectonic plate, stretching from the mid-Atlantic to the West Coast—except for that thin slice of California where the continental and Pacific plates abut, exposing the huge crack in the crust called the San Andreas Fault. While America's interior is mainly a vast ironing board, it is flanked on both coasts by mountain chains. Running parallel to the Atlantic coast are the ancient roller-coaster ranges of the Appalachians, stretching 1,800 miles from Alabama to Newfoundland. Beside the Pacific lies the thrusting backbone of the Cordillera, a belt of steeper, sharper peaks

ranging 5,000 miles from Alaska into Mexico, then towering on majestically through the South American Andes. In North America, the Cordillera is split into two separate chains: the slimmer Coast Ranges, including the Sierra Nevada, Cascade and St. Elias mountains, and the mighty Rockies, nearly 1,000 miles inland.

The Appalachians were created eons ago from the colliding North American and Eurasian-African plates, but their once soaring summits have eroded. The Coast Ranges resulted from the Pacific plate plunging beneath the North American plate, an ongoing process that continues to raise the Sierra Nevada, Cascade and Alaskan ranges. While this subduction also rammed the Canadian Rockies against the continental plate, the American Rockies are mainly a vertical uplift of ancient crust. Between

A lone moose stands against a backdrop of timber and the Brooks Range in Alaska.

the Rockies and Coastal mountains, the crust is still being stretched and split into numerous basins and block ranges.

Across the continent, America's mountains vary drastically, their shape and structure dependent on the geological stresses which thrust them skyward, and the rains, winds and glaciers which sculpted them. Since the Pacific plate is moving northwest, its subduction under Alaska is still shown by recent volcanic activity on the mainland and Aleutian Islands. This coastal chain typifies young mountains on the continent's rim, combining granite cores, metamorphic rocks and volcanoes. The relatively swift uplift of these summits over 10 million years has included both fault-blocking and compression of the crust. The 600-mile, crescent-shaped chain of the Alaska

Range includes glacial valleys and rivers, rumpled lowlands, wide plains, awesome gorges and the highest, most massive peaks on the continent.

Sucking moisture from air sweeping north from the Gulf of Alaska, these mountains produce snow, which compacts into glacial ice. The Alaska Range contains the continent's greatest glacial system, including Mount McKinley, which alone boasts 17 major glaciers, four of them more than 25 miles long. McKinley, at 20,320 feet above sea level, is the highest peak in North America. But because it soars 18,000 feet above its base, it actually dwarfs Mount Everest—considered the world's tallest summit at 29,028 feet above sea level—which in fact rises only 12,000 feet from base to peak.

Moving south, the Cascade Range in the

Latourell Falls is one of many falls found along the precipices of the Columbia Gorge.

Pacific Northwest is a typical volcanic arc formed by the submersion of the oceanic plate beneath the Washington and Oregon coasts, where volcanoes have spewed for 20 million years. While the major volcanic cones such as Mount Hood, Mount St. Helens and Mount Rainier were formed from lava, Mount Triumph's granite and gneiss rocks were thrust to the surface and exposed by erosion. Such solid rocks, so resistant to erosion, tend to form the steepest peaks and sharpest pinnacles.

California's Sierra Nevada, with its long, slanting western slope and steep eastern escarpment, is typical of fault-block ranges, where faulting raised such peaks as Mount Whitney (14,500 feet), and tilted its granite rock to the west. Utah's Wasatch Range, with its stark western face forming the backdrop to Salt Lake City, is one of the continent's largest fault escarpments. Colorado's Rockies were raised from an inland sea—once stretching from the Arctic Ocean to the Gulf of Mexico—which was slowly expelled as the mountains rose in massive blocks to form the core. Sedimentary rocks from the sea once overlaid the granite masses, but eventually folded, buckled and eroded to expose the core. In the San Juan Mountains of Colorado, lava erupting through fissures 20 million years ago covered the older rocks, but left overlying magma rich in gold and silver. Wyoming's Tetons, another recent fault-block range, tower above the basin of Jackson Hole, and have attracted mountaineers for a century.

The Hawaiian mountains are more of a

Early morning light on Whitney Crest, Sierra Nevada, California. (DALE JORGENSON/TOM STACK & ASSOCIATES)

mystery. While scientists know that volcanoes are caused by plate collisions, the Hawaiian islands, while clearly volcanic, are 2,400 miles from the Pacific plate edge. Theorists propose that they lie above a radioactive "hot spot" in the Earth's mantle, hot enough to melt through the moving plate above and spew through the surface. But while the plate continues shifting northeast (at 3 to 5 inches a year), the hot spot remains in place. Thus, the 132 islands (which have surfaced at about 1-million-year intervals) are strung out in a northwest-to-southwest chain, with the oldest at the top and the youngest, Hawaii, at the bottom, where eruptions still occur in its southeast corner. One of these, Mauna Kea, is the highest in the world. While it rises only 13,796 feet above sea level, its total height is 31,796 feet (more than 6 miles) from ocean bed to summit—nearly 2,800 feet taller than Everest.

Meanwhile, as the continental bumper cars keep colliding, the Hawaiian islands will eventually grind against the coasts of Japan or Russia, while chunks of California will break off to join Alaska, thus throwing up the next great mountain ranges. Just as the Appalachians were once in Eastern Europe, North Africa at the South Pole, and Ireland part of Greenland, the map alters inexorably. If the Pacific keeps shrinking as the Atlantic continues to spread, it seems likely that the continents will eventually slide completely around the globe, reforming another supercontinental Pangaea within the Pacific in a mere 200 million years or so.

As the Earth has changed, so have its inhabitants. When land bridges spanned the Bering Strait

Six-hundred-foot-high Bridalveil Fall pours into a misty Yosemite Valley on a spring evening.

Mount Stratton, Vermont, in winter. (GUY MOTIL/FIRST LIGHT)

during the ice ages, countless species of mammals migrated from Asia to North America. Among them was man. By then, though massive glaciers were still moving, the mountain chains stood as they do today; yet even in prehistoric times, the ranges influenced the location of settlements. While the geography of the Cordillera allowed man to migrate from Alaska to beyond the Great Plains, most mountains formed barriers to travel and the mingling of tribes. The Alaska Range halted the hunting forays of the Aleuts. The Adirondacks separated Iroquois and Algonquins. The Sierra Nevada kept Miwoks and Paiutes apart.

Yet the mountains also provided life, the most essential asset being water. Because air is thinner and air pressure lower at high altitudes, there is less air on mountains to hold the heat reflected

from the flatlands, thus temperatures usually drop 1.8°F for every 490 feet in height. So when warm, moist sea winds are deflected upwards, they cool, condense into ice crystals, and fall as snowflakes, therefore capping the highest peaks year round. (The upwind slopes of mountains, where air currents rise, always have higher precipitation than their leeward sides. Tacoma, Washington, for instance, has 37 inches of annual rainfall, while Yakima, 100 miles east across the Cascade Range, averages only 7 inches.) Mountain water also irrigates dense forests, supplying shelter and firewood.

Mountains, as well, have provided food (both alpine peasants and West Coast Indians hunted bighorn sheep and mountain goats), plus minerals. While the natives dug obsidian from the slopes, and white settlers scrambled for

Hikers break for lunch on Mount Mansfield in the Green Mountains, Vermont. (DIANA LAFLEUR/FIRST LIGHT)

copper and silver, the great gold rushes in California, Colorado and the Klondike lured thousands of prospectors into teeming mountain camps. The gold rushes were also a major force in development, since the miners' needs provided economic opportunities for farmers and businessmen.

On the eastern coast, the Appalachians were the first mountains encountered by the European colonists. The great chain—including the Black Mountains of North Carolina, the Great Smokies of Tennessee, the Blue Ridge spine running north from Georgia, the Lehigh, Allegheny and Poconos of Pennsylvania and the Catskills of New York—not only blocked mass migration west, but isolated groups of settlers, fostering the insularity and independence still found within this region. Although New York's Adirondacks

are often considered part of the Appalachians, they are in fact structurally related to Canada's Laurentian Shield.

While 14,000 feet is usually the benchmark of superlatives for big American mountains, most geologists consider one-quarter of Earth's landmass as mountainous—that is, any elevation above 3,000 feet. Around the globe this totals 14 million square miles of mountains, of which 10 percent are high or cold enough to be above the permanent snow line. In New England alone, there are 46 New Hampshire peaks that reach 4,000 feet or higher, 12 more in Maine, five in Vermont and dozens in the Adirondacks. To the early settlers, all were ominous. Yet a few pioneers and their descendants dared to cross them to head west. But far beyond the Great Plains, more ominous ranges loomed.

Many of the Wasatch Range's peaks surpass 11,000 feet.

The first white men to penetrate the western mountains were trappers and fur traders—tough, independent loners. Then came the official explorers, most with military expeditions, whose job it was to study the terrain and find trade routes. In 1804, soon after President Jefferson bought the Louisiana Territory from France, Meriwether Lewis and William Clark led an expedition west to explore the new purchase, crossing the Rockies to reach the Pacific. In 1806, Lieutenant Zebulon Pike was the first American to attempt the ascent of a huge western mountain, and although he failed to even reach its base, Pikes Peak was finally scaled in 1820. Within the next four decades, various geologists and surveyors had climbed most of the highest western summits. By 1870, after numerous Pacific Coast settlements had sprung up, Mount Rainier, Mount Hood and Mount St. Helens had all been surmounted by plucky locals. And then came the true mountaineers.

To primitive man, as Thoreau observed, mountaintops were "sacred and mysterious tracts" on which it would "insult the gods to climb and pry into their secrets. . . . Only daring men climb mountains." Yet, throughout history, daring men have done so. Philip of Macedon ascended Mount Maeumus, Petrarch reached the peak of Mont Ventoux, and Leonardo da Vinci scaled Monte Rosa. Yet it wasn't till the mid-seventeenth century that the first small school of mountaineers began in Zurich, and

Olympic National Park includes part of the Olympic Mountains. (GREG VAUGHN/TOM STACK & ASSOCIATES)

100 years more before Swiss scientist Horace Benedict de Saussure (the father of European mountaineering) climbed Mont Blanc, the highest peak in the Alps, in 1787. His passion was infectious, and soon scores of scientists were exploring alpine summits.

Still, the sport of mountain climbing wasn't established till the mid-nineteenth century, when hordes of affluent Victorians sought escape from the industrial revolution's pressures. The Golden Age of mountaineering, during which many of the customs and techniques of the sport were established, lasted only a decade—from Alfred Wills's famed ascent of the Wetterhorn in 1854, to the successful 1865 assault of the Matterhorn, in which four climbers, including Lord Francis

Douglas, were killed. The tragedy marked not only the scaling of the last great peak of the Alps, but also the end of an era. The tide of mountaineering ebbed for a generation.

While the British went on to their greatest feats after the Second World War—crowned in 1953 by Sir Edmund Hillary's conquest of Everest (on top of which his Sherpa guide, Tenzing Norkay, left a gift of chocolate for the gods)—English climbers had been scaling North America's summits for more than a century. Beginning in British Columbia (with Swiss guides imported by the Canadian Pacific Railway), they transplanted the techniques of the Alps to the Rockies. British botanist David Douglas was scaling American peaks as early as 1827, while an

Colorado's Gore Range extends from Kremmling to Breckenridge, between the Eagle and Blue rivers.
(BRIAN PARKER/TOM STACK & ASSOCIATES)

incredible trio of English clerics climbed Mount Bonney and Mount Assiniboine within the next six decades. Meanwhile, Scottish naturalist John Muir (for whom the massive Muir Glacier is named) led Alaska's first mountain explorations in 1879. As president of the Sierra Club, Muir did more than any man to focus the nation's interest on its mountains. By the twentieth century most of America's major peaks had been surmounted.

Although less than five percent of our planet's surface rises 10,000 feet or higher, 10 percent of all people on Earth live above 3,000 feet. These mountain people adapted their agriculture to the high terrains, and often—like those in the dizzying altitudes and rarefied air of the Andes and Tibetan heights—adapted their bodies as well. But while many see mountains as places to dwell, Americans see them mostly as recreational areas. They go up mountains for the scenery, adventure, danger, challenge. They go to escape, to hike, to fish, to camp, to white-water raft, to climb, but primarily to ski. For many of America's western ski slopes (such as Vail-Beaver Creek, Aspen, Lake Tahoe, Sun Valley, Jackson Hole and Taos) rank with the finest in Europe.

While a zest for adventure—coupled with increased wealth, leisure and vastly improved transportation—is luring more Americans to the mountains, the peaks themselves are infinitely more accessible than they were to the pioneers. Almost all major mountain resorts today are serviced by airports, hairpin highways, railroad

The summit rim of Mount Hood as seen from its upper slopes.

tunnels, cable cars or lifts. (In 1950, 141 climbers struggled to the top of Washington's Mount Rainier. Now more than 4,000 reach the top each year—and another 4,000 try.)

But the government also deserves tremendous credit for protecting America's mountain wilderness by its preservation of nearly 50,000 square miles in 49 national parks. In 1872 an Act of Congress created the 2.2 million acres of Yellowstone National Park (the world's first, and America's largest) to save not only the famous Old Faithful geyser, but thousands of hot springs and mud pools, petrified forests, black grass cliffs, and the nation's richest wildlife preserve outside Alaska. In 1890, both Sequoia and Yosemite in California were also declared parks before President Wilson instituted the Park Service in

1916. The following year, Alaska's Denali National Park was created to protect its teeming wildlife from hunters on the Alaska railroad, and in 1980 Congress tripled its size to 6 million acres. Now each May great herds of caribou cross its tundra for hundreds of miles, over trails worn deep during centuries of migration, to their summer pastures south of the Alaska Range. Among Denali's 200 mammal and bird species, snowy Dall sheep climb its crags, wolf packs roam, grizzlies amble, golden eagles soar, red foxes, hares and lemmings dart, and great bull moose weighing nearly a ton joust each autumn in mating rites.

In the Appalachians, the 180,000 acres of the Great Smoky Mountains National Park was the site of great suffering both before and after its

Dominating the skyline of the Alaska Range is Mount McKinley, North America's highest mountain, at 20,320 feet. (THOMAS KITCHIN/FIRST LIGHT)

formation. One hundred and fifty years ago army troops routed 16,000 peaceable Cherokee Indians from their homes in the hills, and drove them west along the infamous Trail of Tears, on which 4,000 died. (Today, their 8,000 descendants run high stakes bingo on the Qualla Reservation.) Then in 1930 when the park was established, hundreds of mountaineering families who had lived in the Smokies for generations, shooting bear, deer, wild hogs and turkeys and making molasses on mule-turned presses, were also forced to leave. But today, like the tourists, a few old families still return for reunions, to sing hymns, play their fiddles and feast on snap beans, fried chicken and corn bread.

Happily, not all mountain trails were as tragic. Today, millions of Americans and foreign visitors trek across sections of the 2,000-mile-long Appalachian Trail, the longest hiking path in the world. Completed in 1935, it stretches along the Appalachian crest from Mount Oglethorpe in Georgia to Mount Katahdin, Maine, and is one of the continent's most popular vacation spots.

America's mountains—Rainier, Rushmore, McKinley, Mauna Loa, Pole Creek, Pikes Peak—takers of life and sources of great pleasure, born from fire and force, torn from beneath Earth's crust, towering toward heaven. They were here before us, they'll be here when we've gone. Throughout history they have ignited the imagination and stretched the human spirit.

The Elk Mountains, surrounded by the Gunnison and White River national forests, are noted for their mineral deposits and recreational appeal.
(ANNIE GRIFFITHS BELT/FIRST LIGHT)

28

Birches in autumn reflected in Chapel Pond in the Adirondacks, New York.

Mount Baker, the northernmost of the Cascade volcanoes, as seen from the distant San Juan Island, Washington.

Eureka Dune, 700 feet high and itself a small mountain, is located in a desert basin surrounded by desolate peaks.

(Opposite) Wind sculpts the Great Sand Dunes in the foreground of the Sangre de Cristo Mountains.

*The Great Sand Dunes border the San Luis Valley
and the Sangre de Cristo Mountains in Colorado.*

The Guadalupe Mountains overlook a range of cacti.
(MATT BRADLEY/TOM STACK & ASSOCIATES)

Autumn colors highlight trees at the foot of the Maroon Bells, Colorado.

El Capitan, Yosemite's tremendous monolith, seen through the branches of a ponderosa pine in Yosemite Valley, California.

(Opposite) Melting snow still lingers in late July high in the North Cascades, Washington.

A small fraction of the hundreds of acres of forest that were destroyed in the 1980 explosion of Mount St. Helens, Washington.

THE APPALACHIANS

(Opposite) Ferns thrive below a waterfall not far from the Blue Ridge Parkway in North Carolina.

The Little River drains much of the western, Tennessee half of Great Smoky Mountains National Park.

IT HAS BEEN MORE THAN TWO CENturies since Daniel Boone stood on an Appalachian peak to view with "astonishing delight" and a poet's eye, "the ample plains and beauteous tracts below." A later Appalachian explorer, John Muir, mused that "such an ocean of wooded, waving, swelling mountain beauty and grandeur is not to be described." Indeed, since first sighted, the mighty range has stirred such feelings in men's souls.

The Appalachians, which once towered like the Alps till erosion wore them down, are among the oldest uplands on the planet, and few areas on Earth have a richer variety of vegetation. Indeed, among the world's temperate regions, its diversity is unequaled. Within the velvet vistas and bluish haze of the Great Smokies alone are 130 native tree species—far more than in all of Europe—plus more than 1,300 varieties of flowering plants, of which 200 grow nowhere else. In a region that receives the highest rainfall east of the Mississippi, the environment for plant life is ideal. Even Louis XVI sent French botanists to collect the Appalachians' flora.

Yet besides the favorable climate, this neartropical luxuriance is also due to a very richly

Forest canopy near Cades Cove, Great Smoky Mountains National Park, Tennessee. The Great Smokies are notable for sheltering the greatest temperate deciduous forest in existence.

developed soil cover (built up over 60 million years), plus the fact that the mountains escaped the scouring effects of glaciers. Here, in the last great hardwood forests of North America, sweet gums soar to 150 feet, while yellow poplar, or tulip trees, found elsewhere only in China, reach diameters of 11 feet and often tower as high as ten stories before the lowermost limb is reached.

The mountains themselves are as mighty as their trees. In just one small section of North Carolina and Tennessee sit 125 peaks over 5,000 feet. One summit, Mount Le Conte, rises a vertical mile from its valley floor. Yet even Hernando De Soto, who first viewed the range in 1540 and named it after the Gulf Coast Apalachee tribe, could not have known how expansive the Appalachians were. Rising up to 6,642 feet and stretching over 17 degrees of the Earth's curvature, their thousand pinnacles overlook 100,000 square miles of scenery. Even today's famous Appalachian Trail runs for 2,000 miles across 14 states and takes 5 million paces to traverse, although few hikers ever have walked the entire distance.

But even on side trails strollers will find such legendary watering holes as Stink or Panther Creek, Podunk Brook, Female or Surplus Pond, Buttermilk Falls and Mooselookmeguntic Lake. They'll see mountains called Chunky Gal, Blood, Big Bald, Blue Ridge, Nesuntabunt, Slaughter

Fall Creek Falls in the Cumberland Mountains of Tennessee is the highest free-leaping waterfall east of the Rockies.

Mountain laurel make a showy display in the Cumberland Mountains of Tennessee in early May.

and Music, or trails named Fishin' Jimmy, Racoon Branch, Six Husbands, Skookumchuck and Rocky Row Run Road. They'll pass places named Roaring Fork, Buzzards Rock, Breezy Point, Devils Den, Dogtail Corners, Angels Rest, Jobildunk Ravine, Humpback Rocks, Potato Top, Cuckoo Lookout, Devils Pulpit, and gaps called Gooch, Spy Run, Devils Fork, Lost Spectacles and Sassafras.

Each name has a story, each is rooted in history and legend because every era of American history has involved the Appalachians area: Indian, explorer, colonist, settler, soldier, mountain man. The Cherokees camped and trekked through its forest vastness long before the Spanish ever saw it. And its mountain people were part of the first white immigrant stock to

settle the English-speaking New World. During the 1760s, Daniel Boone crossed the Blue Ridge mountains on hunting expeditions. After an Indian attack while he was blazing a trail through the Cumberland Gap, Boone led a band of armed colonists through this corridor, then began to colonize Kentucky in defiance of the British. Three days after the Battle of Lexington, the fort at Boonesborough flew the flag of the new colony of Transylvania.

During the Revolutionary War, Irish and Scottish settlers arrived in Tennessee to build farmsteads in the Appalachian Valley and surrounding hillside hamlets. The first Americans to cut loose from the Atlantic seaboard, these Appalachian frontiersmen were also the first to establish governments in defiance of the king.

Mountain laurel blooms in the Appalachian Mountains of Shenandoah National Park, Virginia.

Equipped with muskets at their own expense, the superb marksmen swept down from their corn patches and defeated Cornwallis at Yorktown. At war's end, skirmishes continued for years with Indians who controlled the southern Appalachian passes. Treaties were signed, but rarely observed. Though the Cherokees were loyal to the United States during the War of 1812, they were stripped of their property after Andrew Jackson's election and finally forced into mass exodus.

Although troops had opened routes through the mountains, much of the terrain remained unsurveyed. In 1857, Professor Elisha Mitchell made a solitary trek to determine which Appalachian peak was the highest. After his body was discovered at the base of what is now named Mount Mitchell, Senator Thomas Clingman led an expedition to establish Clingmans Dome as the tallest peak in the Smokies.

For the Appalachian hillbillies, however, who cared less about mountain measurements, the nineteenth century stood still. They spoke a dialect described as "Elizabethan English," excelled as natural singers and balladists, showed warm hospitality to strangers, and retained a European taste for liquid distilled from grain. After they discovered that Indian corn (which flourished on the mountain slopes) produced mash which, after distillation, gave "a divine jolt when it passes the esophagus," the art of moonshining flourished—illegally, of course, since thrifty Scots immigrants saw no reason to pay stiff taxes on store-bought libations. They

In May the valleys have been lush green for weeks, while along the high, cool crest of the Blue Ridge mountains the deciduous trees are still in bud.

(Opposite) Grasses above the timberline on the summit of Algonquin Peak in the Adirondacks turn gold in the autumn.

built their stills beside swift streams, and planted their corn on slopes so steep they had to prop the stalks with rocks.

The government paid scant attention to the practice until 1876—when it discovered that 3,000 illicit stills were operating in Appalachia. Revenue agents were naturally repulsed; some were shot. The white lightning war continued for a century. In 1956, T-men smashed 14,000 stills. In 1972, they still found 2,981. Yet the sympathetic public chuckled when a moonshiner said, "We-uns hain't no call to be ashamed of ourselves. We stay way up hyer in these coves, and mind our own dang business."

Today, with the advent of highways and tourists, few of the traditional mountain customs are preserved, but the Appalachian people remain as proud and independent as their ancestors. For this is the land where Boone fought, Davy Crockett hunted, Thomas Jefferson lived, Stonewall Jackson led his Rebs toward the Shenandoah, Ethan Allen galloped his raiders into Vermont, Henry David Thoreau and Walt Whitman wrote, Robert Frost penned poetry, and mountain men brewed "co'n whiskey." When a hiker asked one hillbilly hoeing his patch, "How do I get down from here?" the grizzled oldster croaked, "Don't know. I was borned here. Never bin there."

For to those who lived in the Appalachians, there was nowhere else on Earth.

(Opposite) Autumn colors on the flank of Giant Mountain in the Adirondacks, New York.

Mount Lafayette, the highest in the Franconia Range of the White Mountains, New Hampshire.

Part of the great forest floral display of the Blue Ridge mountains, rhododendron frame Linville Falls, North Carolina.

Spring forest below Clingmans Dome, the highest mountain in Tennessee, in Great Smoky Mountains National Park.

The Great Smoky Mountains, seen here at dusk from the Foothills Parkway, are named for the mists that so frequently settle between the heavily forested ridges.

(Opposite) The highest peaks in the east are found in the Blue Ridge mountains of North Carolina, seen here from near the end of the Blue Ridge Parkway.

A view from Mount Washington in New Hampshire's White Mountains. It is the highest of the northeastern peaks and has the most extensive area above timberline.

There are over a thousand miles of trails within the White Mountain National Forest, giving hikers an endless variety to choose from. (SCOTT LESLIE/FIRST LIGHT)

Cows graze in this pastoral scene of the Appalachians.
(GARRY BRIAND/FIRST LIGHT)

(Opposite) An aerial view of one of Mount Katahdin's peaks.

THE COAST RANGES
AND ROCKY MOUNTAINS

(Opposite) The granite monolith of El Capitan rises 3,614 feet above Yosemite Valley. (PAUL VON BAICH/FIRST LIGHT)

Half Dome in late afternoon light with Clouds Rest behind in shadow, Yosemite National Park.

HISTORY'S GREATEST ERUPTION occurred 600,000 years ago when Yellowstone blew, hurtling hundreds of cubic miles of earth as far east as Kansas, and leaving a crater 50 miles wide and half a mile deep. The more recent eruption of Mount St. Helens in 1980, one of the most violent ever known, only proves once again that mountains are never permanent.

Both peaks are part of the great Pacific Cordillera, stretching 5,000 miles from Alaska into Mexico, and split into two separate chains: the Coast Ranges, which includes Mount St. Helens,

and the Rockies, where Yellowstone's Old Faithful still spouts. The Cordillera was born when the North American and Pacific plates collided, and mountains began rising from the impact. Then, during the ice ages, man began crossing the Bering Strait to live along the ranges. Skeletal remains and chiseled flint dating back 50,000 years have been found in California.

First came the hunters of deer and elk, with dogs as their only pack animals. The Spaniards arrived in the 1500s, bringing horses. Then came such great explorers as Alexander Mackenzie, whose

Lupines on Klahhane Ridge in Olympic National Park, Washington. (SHARON GERIG/TOM STACK & ASSOCIATES)

(Opposite) Colorful alpine flowers form the foreground for Mount Rainier. (F. STUART WESTMORLAND/TOM STACK & ASSOCIATES)

expeditions led to such rival enterprises as the North West and Hudson's Bay companies with their Indian trading posts. Beginning in the 1800s, they were followed by the fabled mountain men, who trapped beaver in every mountain stream. For two feverish decades beginning in 1825, more than 1,000 nomadic trappers roamed the Rockies (of whom at least 180 were slain by Indians). Then came the first settlers, followed by the Mormons in 1847, who had barely erected homesteads when the California Gold Rush of 1849 began. Until then, most travelers to the Rockies were transients, but that changed forever when a decade later gold and silver were discovered in Colorado.

In the spring of 1879, for example, Leadville,

Colorado, was the fastest-growing boomtown in America. It was only 12 months younger than the 3-year-old state, but its merchants, prospectors and prostitutes were becoming overnight millionaires on silver strikes. H.A.W. Tabor, a grocer whose $17 grubstake had shot him to a $20-million fortune (and marriage to the legendary beauty Baby Doe), was erecting a gilded, crystal-chandeliered opera house between the honky-tonk saloons and dance halls.

Yet recent arrivals were restless. Most of the claims were already staked. The only riches left, they surmised, were over the Rockies to the west, across the Great Divide. But the Divide not only split the continent—and the runoff of rivers to the Atlantic or Pacific—it formed the

Sunrise on Mount Shasta, the second highest of the Cascade volcanoes and, with its summit glaciers, the only perpetually white peak in California.

spiny demarcation between white and Indian country. To the east was Denver and civilization. To the west were grizzlies, the highest altitude in the nation, and the rampaging Ute Indian tribe. Men knew that death lay over the mountains. Still, in June that year two groups of sourdoughs left Leadville and trekked 70 miles over the Sawatch Range into Independence Pass. And there, between Aspen and Smuggler mountains, by the banks of the Roaring Fork river, they found traces of ore and staked claims. Though none of them knew it, they'd discovered one of the richest silver lodes in history.

The prospectors built a dozen log cabins, called their settlement Ute City, and soon other miners trickled in. But then, in early October, a rider came crashing in from Glenwood Springs, 40 miles upriver, with terrifying news. The Utes had murdered the local Indian agent and 11 men, and taken their women. Another band had massacred a U.S. troop riding in from Wyoming. The courier warned them to flee. Only two stayed behind. The tiny settlement seemed doomed at birth. Then, miraculously, a few weeks later, the Ute chief, Ouray, signed a truce and sourdoughs poured back in. However, by winter, all but 13 returned again to the comforts of Leadville. One man sold his claim, called the Smuggler, for $50 and a mule. (A decade later the Smuggler poured out millions.)

By the following March, however, parties were again crossing the pass on snowshoes. Some led

Mount Rainier, Washington, the grandest mountain outside of Alaska, has numerous glaciers.

cows and carried zithers. The trails resembled the Klondike Gold Rush. And, as in the Klondike, many died. Some were buried in avalanches, others starved, still others froze. Many became snow-blind, but the line moved on. A man named Gillespie built Norwegian snow boats on 8-foot skis, loaded them with 200 pounds of supplies, and pulled them at night when the snow was hard. By summer, he was wrapping 1,000-pound lots of ore in cowhides and rolling the bundles down Aspen Mountain to be shipped to the Leadville smelter. He got four cents a pound—and fabulously rich.

By then Ute City had been renamed Aspen after the white-barked trees with silver leaves that smother its lower slopes. For the next ten years, the valley spewed out silver ore. One pocket alone, the size of a woodshed, produced $500,000. A silver nugget weighing a ton had to be sliced into thirds to squeeze it out of Smuggler. But mule trains couldn't haul the ore out fast enough. Although smelters and crushing plants were built, ore sat stacked in the streets like giant gray snowdrifts until two railroads pushed through in 1887. Soon 14 trains a day were chugging up from Denver, bringing hundreds of fortune hunters. By 1890 there were 12,000 inhabitants, 70 bars, 20 hotels, 10 churches, six newspapers, three banks, three schools, a courthouse and bustling brothel district. Aspen was the first town in Colorado to have a polo field and to run entirely on electricity. More than 100 light-opera

Mount Whitney, the highest peak in the lower forty-eight states, from Lone Pine, California.

(Opposite) The Garden of the Gods below Pikes Peak, Colorado, was formed by the erosion of vertical layers of sandstone, which were originally upturned during the raising of the Rockies.

players were brought from Vienna to fill the new $90,000 opera house. Huge Victorian mansions were erected, and everyone grew rich. Aspen's silver lodes produced a staggering quarter of a billion dollars.

Then in July, 1893, disaster struck when the United States went onto the gold standard. Aspen was devastated. Banks failed, mines shut, 1,800 miners were jobless. Most moved on to the new goldfields in Idaho. By 1914, Aspen had become a ghost town. The remaining 700 citizens survived by supplying farmers and ranchers in the valley. The elegant homes, hotels and theaters were left to the dust. The bonanza was dead.

But, as every modern skier knows, the slopes and snows that once slew the sourdoughs proved to be Aspen's salvation. Since the 1950s its real estate value has run rampant. Today, with more than 100 bistros, beds for 11,000 guests, more resident movie stars than Beverly Hills and 300 miles of incredible ski trails, Aspen has gone from ghost town to boomtown once again in less than 40 years. The spa, set high in the Rockies, is one of the world's most famous resorts.

Grand Prismatic Hot Spring is one of the largest and most colorful in Yellowstone National Park, Wyoming.

The glacier-sculpted basin of Cirque of the Towers has some of the most striking scenery in the Wind River Range, Wyoming.

(Previous pages) Grand Teton, the famous summit of Grand Teton National Park, Wyoming.

Mount McKinley in Alaska, one of the greatest mountains, is the highest in the world above its snowline.

Moonrise and Mount Sanford, a volcano that is the highest summit in the Wrangell Mountains, Alaska.

Alpine flowers sown by the wind carpet the hillsides of Glacier National Park.

*River-incised tundra at the base of the Alaska Range,
Denali National Park, Alaska.*

(Previous pages) Sunrise at Cirque of the Towers, Wind River Range, Wyoming.

Fresh snowfall in September in the Sawtooth Wilderness of Idaho, a region with many small lakes and very jagged granite pinnacles.

Alaska Basin is a secluded backpacking destination on the west slope of the Tetons in Grand Teton National Park.

Colorado's Sawatch Range is the highest section of the Rockies.

Icefields in the St. Elias mountains on the Yukon-Alaska border.

The Matanuska Glacier is in Alaska's Chugach Mountains, which extend from Cook Inlet to the St. Elias mountains.

The mountain goat, an animal that is well adapted to steep terrain, is one of many wildlife species found in Montana's Glacier National Park.

Denali National Park, Alaska, one of the most pristine wilderness areas, consists mostly of mountainous terrain and trailless tundra.

The jagged Arrigetch Peaks in Alaska's Brooks Range derived their name from an Inuit word meaning "fingers of the hand extended."

(Opposite) Precambrian gneiss, a metamorphic rock, in Rocky Mountain National Park, Colorado.

The view from Trail Ridge in Rocky Mountain National Park, Colorado.

(Previous pages) The Sawatch Range looms in the distance over Colorado's Black Canyon of the Gunnison National Monument.

The San Juan Mountains were created as a result of a gigantic volcanic episode about 40 million years ago.

The unusual coloration of the Grand Canyon of Yellowstone is due to heat-altered rhyolite, an acidic volcanic rock.

*The intricate channels of a braided river in Alaska
are formed by heavy loads of silt and gravel that are
carried by the water from their glacial source.*

Shadows and boulders provide graphic contrast on the snow-covered slopes of Alaska's Kenai Mountains.

A grizzly forages in early snow in Yellowstone National Park, Wyoming.

*The Alaska Range, Denali National Park, has im-
mense glaciers draining from Mount McKinley and
Mount Foraker.*

(Opposite) Bare granite, gnarled trees and bushes gilded in autumn below Kindersley Pass in the eastern Sierra Nevada, California.

Multnomah Falls is the highest of a considerable number of falls in the Columbia Gorge, Oregon.

*Spring runoff streaks some of the many cliffs around
Yosemite Valley, including these above Vernal Fall.*

Cumulus clouds, reminiscent of summer, build over the Ritter Range while even in late May the high country of the Minarets Wilderness in California's Sierra Nevada remains snowbound.

96

A treeless landscape amid 14,000-foot peaks greets the traveler at Forester Pass along the John Muir Trail in the Sierra Nevada, California.

(Opposite) A clump of pearly everlasting is among the sparse growth that is beginning to reclaim slopes that were devastated in the explosion of Mount St. Helens.

At 594 feet, Nevada Fall on the Merced River is the most powerful, but certainly not the highest waterfall in Yosemite Valley, California.

*Sunset above Cascade Pass in North Cascades
National Park, Washington.*

100

Pearly everlasting is among the abundant and varied flowers at Cascade Pass, North Cascades National Park, Washington.

Phlox adds to the colorful slopes of Mount Rainier, Washington, where some of the most profusely flowered alpine meadows in the world are found.

(Opposite) The east escarpment of the Sierra Nevada rises beyond sagebrush and lava beds south of Bishop, California.

Mount Olympus is the highest in northwest Washington's Olympic mountain range.

A mountain wall detail in the Brooks Range, Alaska.

A ptarmigan's summer plumage is perfect camouflage against rock, grass and lichen in the Colorado Rockies.

(Previous pages) Oregon's Crater Lake lies within an extinct volcano. (BILL ROSS/FIRST LIGHT)

The Sangre de Cristo Mountains (the name means "blood of Christ" in Spanish) are so called because of the reddish hue of their peaks at sunset.
(SPENCER SWANGER/TOM STACK & ASSOCIATES)

The Brooks Range forms a backdrop for the foaming waters of Arrigetch Creek in Alaska.

HAWAII

(Opposite) Kilauea crater in Hawaii Volcanoes National Park is unpredictable in its explosions. Viewed at night, Kilauea's lava flow is a mesmerizing cascade of color. (KEN SAKAMOTO/FIRST LIGHT)

The steep, fluted mountains of Kauai are breathtaking, particularly when viewed from a beach below. (RON WATTS/FIRST LIGHT)

HAWAII'S VOLCANIC MOUNTAINS were already standing when the first Polynesians arrived around 700 A.D., followed by the Marquesans. For nearly five centuries the two tribes lived in harmony, until, in the twelfth century, the Tahitians stormed in and forced their customs, language and religion on the settlers. And among them, some say, was a girl named Pele, who arrived with her sisters. Renowned throughout the islands as a beautiful sorceress, she was suddenly engulfed in an eruption of lava, and returned as Hawaii's goddess of fire.

Others believe Pele actually created the volcanoes. One legend says the goddess came long ago to escape her evil sister, Na Maka, and was poking out the crater on Niihau to hide in when her sister found her. Pele then fled on to Kauai, Oahu, Molokai, Lanai and Maui—digging even deeper as she was pursued—until finally she scooped out the great crater of Halemaumau in Kilauea, where she

The distant Kohala Mountains are in the northwestern region of Hawaii. (JANET DWYER/FIRST LIGHT)

now lives safely in her impenetrable fortress. Another legend claims that Pele created the islands while searching for a perfect home. After she finally arrived at Kilauea with the handsome high chief, Lohiau, he fell in love with her younger sister, Hiiaka. Furiously, Pele engulfed them both in lava. But when Lohiau breathed her name before dying, Pele promised to build another island for them both to live in. And today, a new island named Loihi is indeed arising. Thirty miles south of Kilauea, it stands 16,000 feet above the ocean floor, just 3,000 feet below the surface, and erupted as recently as 1980.

While the legends vary, all islanders know that the fire goddess Pele is still alive and living in Halemaumau crater in Kilauea, the living center of Hawaii's volcanic activity, as well as the most active volcano on Earth. Along with the famous volcanoes of Mauna Kea and Mauna Loa, Kilauea's crater (with an 11-mile hike around its rim) is today the heart of Hawaii Volcanoes National Park.

After the Tahitian invasion of Hawaii the islands returned to total isolation. Lying in the central Pacific, 2,400 miles from North America and 3,000 miles from all land to the west, they remained forgotten for nearly 500 years. Then on January 20, 1778, the Pacific's greatest explorer, Captain James Cook, set foot on Kauai with his 112 men (including George Vancouver

The extinct volcano of Mauna Kea, which translates from Hawaiian as "white mountain," has snow from December to April. (CHUCK O'REAR/FIRST LIGHT)

and William Bligh). Greeted at first as a god, Cook was killed a year later in Kelakekua Bay when, after racing into the surf to escape a hostile mob, he stood, helplessly surrounded, because he couldn't swim.

But Cook's discovery of the islands brought Hawaii into the modern world. By 1790, King Kamehameha had conquered the entire archipelago and united it into a nation when the first whalers and traders arrived, followed by the missionaries, who went to smash idols, save souls and civilize. Many natives have never forgiven them for succeeding so well, since their descendants now own most of Hawaii's corporate empires.

After King Kamehameha II and his queen died of measles in London in 1824, their son ruled for 30 years. During his reign, the Japanese, Chinese and Filipinos began arriving, just as whaling died out and the great sugarcane plantations began. The last reigning monarch, Queen Liliuokalani, was removed in 1893 in a bloodless uprising, and replaced in power by Sanford Dole of pineapple fame. Yet, while under house rule she wrote the poignant song of goodbye, "Aloha Oe," which was also a lament for past glory when kings, queens and gods walked the islands.

Today, the chain of 132 volcanic islands, reefs and atolls—stretching 1,600 miles in

114

Waimea Canyon, often called the Grand Canyon of the Pacific, has red and ocher coloration that contrasts with the green vegetation in its hollows.
(RON WATTS/FIRST LIGHT)

(Opposite) Lush agricultural land in the Hanalei Valley, Kauai. (RON WATTS/FIRST LIGHT)

length—comprises the most visited 6,424 square miles on Earth. Each year armies of tourists flock to such famous landmarks as Waikiki, Diamond Head and the 10,023-foot-high Haleakala crater, the crown of Maui, which last erupted in 1790. Towering above the 28,665 acres of Haleakala National Park, the world's largest dormant volcanic crater covers 19 square miles in area, stretches 21 miles in circumference and plunges 3,000 feet from its summit. To enter it is like stepping on the moon. Its 32 miles of trails crisscross crater cones, strewn volcanic rubble, vents and frozen lava flows, from which hikers chip off chunks.

But visitors carting off souvenir rocks from Hawaii Volcanoes National Park risk the full

blast of Pele's fury. Since every part of the Kilauea volcano is a piece of Pele—a fingernail, lock of hair, earlobe—tourists who take samples home may suffer everything from smashed teacups to broken legs, which is why each month park rangers receive dozens of boxes of rocks, sheepishly sent back.

Pele lives!

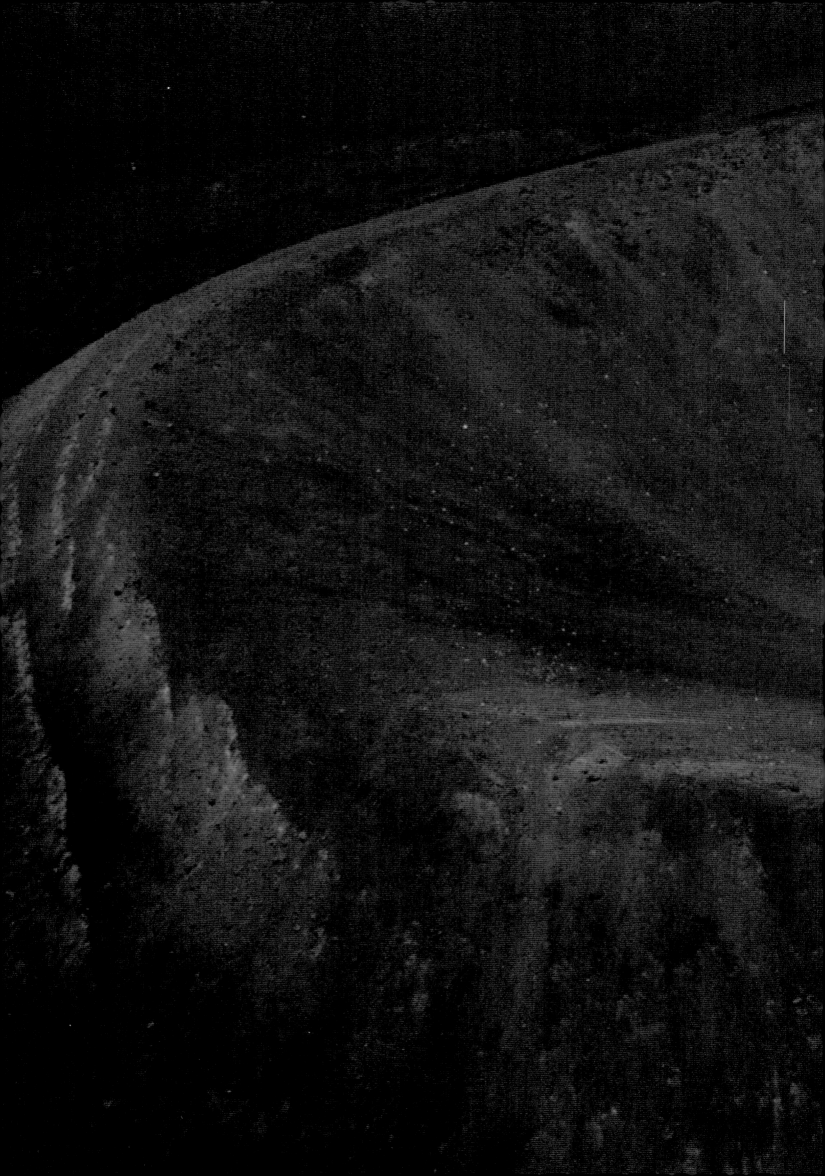

(Previous pages) Haleakala Crater and a sizable portion of surrounding land were made into a national park in 1916 to preserve this fine example of a dormant volcano. (ARTURO A. WESLEY)

A silversword plant gleams in the moonlight on the slope of Haleakala Crater, Hawaii. (RON WATTS/FIRST LIGHT)

These sharply contoured cliffs along the Na Pali Coast
form part of Hawaii's diverse terrain.
(ALVIS VOITIS/THE IMAGE BANK)

The 10,023-foot dormant Haleakala crater dominates the landscape of Maui. (RON WATTS/FIRST LIGHT)